The Amazing Quantum

Five Awesome Stories of People Who Made a Revolution in Physics

Nury Vittachi
Illustrations by Step Cheung

Contents

THE BOY WHO DIDN'T LISTEN TO HIS TEACHER

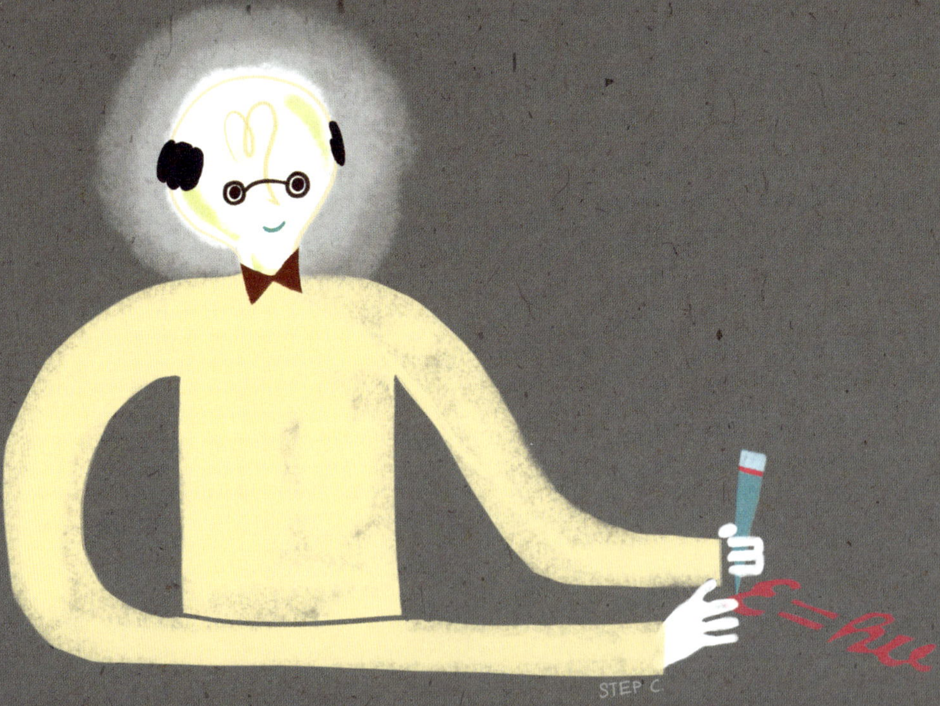

A TEENAGE BOY HAD a problem. Like many students, Max had a favorite subject. But his teacher told him there was no future in his area of interest, which was physics. It was the late 1800s and scientists had found everything there was to be found.

"In this field, almost everything is already discovered, and all that remains is to fill a few holes," said his teacher Philipp von Jolly.

Boo! What a shame. Max Planck loved physics and felt that he would have loved to have gone on to be a scientist, discovering lots of important new things.

But what else could he do? Max was also very good at music — he could sing well, and played many different instruments. So that was an option.

Max was quite a spiritual boy, and in the end he decided to go with what he felt called to do in his heart: he chose to stay with physics, against the advice of his own science teacher.

He did well in his studies at university, and soon became a professor of physics — that "finished" line of investigation.

One day an electrical company asked Professor Planck to help them improve their light bulbs. This was the 1890s, and electric lights had become popular in Europe.

At that time, scientists were very puzzled about the nature of light, but could make no progress in their attempts to understand it better.

Max looked at how light worked and eventually had a brainwave. Light energy comes in little tiny pieces, too small to see, he realized. He named the parts using the Latin word for piece, which is "quantum".

At that stage in history, most people thought light was a wave, so his idea was quite revolutionary.

Despite the simplicity of the idea, it turned out to be a notion that would turn science upside down.

That year, 1900, he was walking in the snow with one of his children, and he revealed that he had discovered something that might make him famous, like Isaac Newton. He was right.

Many other people, including Albert Einstein, one of the most famous scientists of all time, joined Planck in investigating this new discovery and the result was "quantum mechanics" — a new branch of study that soon became the dominant part of physics.

One of the strangest discoveries was that REALITY ITSELF is made up of tiny individual pieces which have a minimum size, like pixels.

If you take a piece of nothing, you can break it down only to a certain size, now called "Planck's Length". (The size, in meters, is "1.6162 x 10 to the power of minus 35". Think of it as a decimal point followed by 35 zeroes before you get to the actual numbers.)

These tiny elements of space make up reality in the same way that pixels make up the picture on your computer screen. It's a strange thought, isn't it?

Usually, it's good for students to listen to their teachers. But in this case, it was a good thing Max Planck didn't!

HOW A COMPASS INSPIRED A GENIUS

ONE DAY, A DAD CALLED Hermann showed something to his little boy.

It was a compass. Compasses are interesting things. The needle moves around as you walk around. But it always ends up pointing in a certain direction. "It's showing us the way to the North Pole," Hermann said.

The little boy, whose name was Al, and who was about eight years old at the time, stared at the device in amazement.

Holding the compass in his hand, he turned himself in circles — but the needle always settled down to point in the same direction.

E=mc²

Most children are intrigued the first time they see a compass, but soon forget it.

But not Al. He was a puzzle solver. He needed to know why it did what it did. It was clear to him that some powerful invisible force existed in the world, and the compass was a clue to its existence. He was determined to find out what it was and how it worked.

The boy, whose full name was Albert Einstein, soon took up a hobby of building mechanical things for fun.

But his father Hermann was not very successful with his electrical engineering business in his home country, Germany, so the whole family moved to Italy to find new customers. This was in the 1800s.

When Al was about 14, he wrote a short essay about science. It was called: "On the Investigation of the State of the Ether in a Magnetic Field."

Clearly, magnetic power, like the force that moved compass needles, needed to move all the way from the North Pole to the compass in his Dad's hand. But how? Did it jump from molecule to molecule?

No. Scientists already knew that magnetic forces could travel through a vacuum, which is a patch of emptiness containing nothing, no molecules, not even air.

At that time, 1894, people decided there must be an invisible substance in empty air. They called it "the ether". It had to exist to carry things such as magnetic forces and light particles.

But no one at the time ever found any of it.

Albert Einstein became very famous — one of the most famous scientists in history. He made his most important discoveries when he was a young man — with four discoveries in his 26th year alone.

He learned that the ether, as it was thought of in those days, did not exist. But there DID exist something called space-time, which we can think of as the basic "stuff" of which reality is made. Some people think of space-time as a sort of "super ether".

Other scientists have come to agree that the ether is actually a useful concept, although these days we use other names for it, such as "vacuum energy" or even "the grid".

Einstein and Planck and their colleagues confirmed that even empty space is made of elements which can be thought of as pixels — little grainy pieces of reality: what an amazing thought!

STEP C.

THE BOY SECRETLY READING A BOOK BEHIND HIS SCHOOL DESK

TEACHER LOOKED AT HIS CLASS. As usual, some of the students were paying attention; some were not.

There was one boy in particular, whose name was Wolfgang, who seemed uninterested in what was being taught.

Instead, Wolfgang would sit with his head tilted forward. He was reading something he was holding behind his desk.

How did the teachers at school react to Wolfgang?

You'd think they would be angry, and probably some were, at first.

But in the end, Wolfgang didn't get into trouble. That's because the teachers discovered exactly what Wolfgang liked to read behind his desk. It was Albert Einstein's writings about relativity!

These are a pair of scientific documents which are famous for being VERY difficult to understand.

It soon became clear that the reason why Wolfgang did not pay attention at school is that the lessons were far too easy for him.

He quickly understood what was being taught, and was hungry for more information, which he was finding himself.

This scene, of Wolfgang reading in secret behind his desk, happened about 100 years ago in Germany. Einstein wrote about relativity in two works, one of which was published in 1905, and another in 1916.

The boy, Wolfgang Pauli, read the works with great interest — even though they were so complicated that very few adults could understand what they were saying.

In these works, Einstein explained that reality was not what we thought it was. It could be thought of as a physical thing called space-time. And it could be shaped, or bent, or curved, by gravity. Even things that moved in straight lines, such as beams of light, could be shaped by gravity.

These were stunning ideas, and Wolfgang was fascinated.

It turned out that the teachers were right to let Wolfgang do things his own way.

The boy left school to go to university while still young, and finished his degree at the age of 18 (which is, of course, the age that most university students start their degrees).

Three years later, Wolfgang wrote an important work. Einstein himself wrote a note about it: "Whoever studies this mature and grandly conceived work might not believe that its author is a 21-year-old man."

Wolfgang Pauli went on to become one of the most important scientists of the modern age. He worked on what are called the "fundamental particles" — this means the smallest pieces of matter, the little tiny things that make up everything in the world.

Even though these particles are too small to see, young scientist Pauli managed to deduce some important details about them, and is considered one of the fathers of quantum physics, the most influential set of findings in science in the past 100 years.

This does NOT mean that you, dear reader, should stop paying attention to your teachers and secretly read things behind your desk. (Unless, perhaps, it is science class and you are keeping your enthusiasm high by reading this book!)

THE STUDENT WHOSE SCHOOLS KEPT CLOSING

IF YOU GET A DAY off school, you're pretty happy, right?

But what if you felt that you were born to be a science scholar but fate kept stopping you from going to school?

That was the problem of a boy called T. D. Lee, who loved books and learning.

Lee Tsung Dao lived in Shanghai when World War II broke out. China was invaded and his school was closed down.

So the boy who loved studying left school without any qualifications.

But luckily, he managed to persuade the professors at Zhejiang University to let him join. It may be that his love of studying showed in his eyes.

Then his luck turned bad again. There was another invasion of China (the war was still continuing) and now his university was forcibly shut down!

Poor T. D. Lee. He must have felt that destiny was angry with him, which seemed unfair. He was a hardworking young student, and his family were good, well-respected people. (His grandfather was the rector of a very famous church in Suzhou.)

But it turned out that fate, secretly, had big plans for T. D. Lee. The interruption of his university studies meant that he had to move to Kunming, where he met a man called Professor Wu Ta-You, who nominated him for a Chinese government fellowship to study in the USA.

In 1946, T. D. went to Chicago and met a famous scientist, Professor Enrico Fermi, who noticed that the youngster was totally devoted to becoming a science scholar. The Professor chose T. D. as a researcher.

Professor Fermi was one of the world leaders in modern physics. And that meant T. D. had a close-up view of the cutting-edge puzzles in science.

At that time, scientists had noticed an intriguing fact. It seemed that reality, at its deepest level, might be reversible: every process that went one way could also go the other way.

They called this Parity Symmetry.

Most non-scientists said this was not true. How can every process be reversible? You cannot take the milk out of your coffee, nor can you turn a scrambled egg back into an uncooked egg.

But scientists said that at the level of atoms, it may be that you can reverse all processes.

Yet how could this be tested? No one knew how.

T. D. Lee and a colleague, Yang Chen-Ning, worked out a way to test this using tiny particles. He worked out that all the particle interactions which make up reality were symmetrical, except for one. It was such an unexpected answer that it soon got all the top physicists around the world talking about it.

He and his colleague C. N. Yang were given the Nobel Prize in 1957. T. D. was just 30 years old. (The woman who worked in the lab, running the experiments, also became famous — but that's another story, which you can find in Book 2 of this series, Fabulous Physics.)

So the boy who thought that fate did not want him to be a science scholar ended up being celebrated as one of the greatest science scholars of the century.

α = β = μ = 180
1+2+3+4+5+6
A-C/C = D
e = cosx + tgy
√a² = |a|
E = MC²
a² + b² = c²
STEPC

THE BOY WHO HAD A DISPUTE WITH HIS FATHER

ONCE THERE WAS A BOY called Jancsi who had an amazing ability to keep numbers in his head.

But his dad complained: "You'll never earn any money doing mathematics. You should be a businessman instead."

You would not believe how good little Jancsi was when handling pages of numbers.

When guests came to the house of the von Neumann family, Jancsi's father, a banker named Max, would call his son to perform.

"Watch this," Max would say. He would open the telephone book at a random page and hand it to his son. The child, who was just six years old, would read it.

Then the adults would pass around the book and read out names or addresses from that page.

Jancsi would tell them the corresponding phone number, showing that he remembered everything on the whole page.

The boy could do mental maths too, easily dividing pairs of eight-digit numbers in his head.

The family lived in Budapest, Hungary, during the time of the First World War. They were Jewish, so life was dangerous.

But they survived the war, and when the boy was 15, a famous mathematician was brought to the house to give him extra lessons. The teacher was so astonished at the teenager's ability that he burst into tears, moved to be in the presence of a genius.

But when it was time for Jancsi to go to university, the trouble started at home. He wanted to do a top university qualification, a PhD, in mathematics.

But his father wanted him to be a businessman. "There's no money in mathematics," he said.

"Do something practical, like science."

What was Jancsi to do?

Jancsi himself came up with the answer. He announced that he would sign up at two universities at once and do two degrees at once — one in mathematics, and one in chemistry.

And so he did.

His mathematics teacher at university was astonished at his student. Whenever he would mention an unsolved problem in the world of calculations, the boy would immediately scribble down the answer.

These were not just test questions, but major problems that professional mathematicians were struggling with.

Well, in the long run, it turned out that Jancsi's father was wrong.

The boy, under his formal name of John von Neumann, became a super-famous mathematician.

And he did earn good money. In fact, he ended by sharing a university department with Albert Einstein, one of the smartest people ever.

John von Neumann's mathematics was so powerful they needed it for quantum physics.

And when important new inventions were created, such as the atom bomb, scientists would call Jancsi (in the USA they called him "Johnny") to come and be in charge of the maths.

He was paid A LOT of money. His dad should really have trusted him!

KEEP READING

READING ABOUT THE LIVES of scientists and other discoverers adds to our store of knowledge, but we hope also leads us towards something much greater, which is wisdom.

This book is part of a series, which we hope you'll enjoy reading, and will spur you on to do your own scientific research.

The creators of this book wish you success in your explorations.

THE YOUNG SCIENTISTS SERIES

Book 1: SECRETS IN THE ROCKS
Five Astounding Tales of People Solving Mysteries Beneath Our Feet

Book 2: FABULOUS PHYSICS
Five Amazing Stories of People Who Solved Nature's Puzzles

Book 3: MAGICAL MATHEMATICS
Five Astonishing Stories of People Who Did Miracles with Numbers

Book 4: BREAKERS OF BARRIERS
Five Stunning Stories of People Demolishing Walls to Make History

Book 5: SCIENTIFIC PIONEERS
Five Incredible Tales of People Who Helped Develop the Scientific Method

Book 6: THE AMAZING QUANTUM
Five Awesome Stories of People Who Made a Revolution in Physics

Book 7: THE SCIENCE OF HUMANITY
Five Fascinating Stories of People Who Helped Us Understand Ourselves

Book 8: WOMEN OF DISCOVERY
Five Super Stories of Fabulous Females Who Made Scientific History

Book 9: THE INVENTOR'S SPARK
Five Marvelous Stories of People Who Helped Shape the Modern World

Book 10: ADVANCES IN ALCHEMY
Five Startling Stories of Chemistry and Biology

Book 11: THE CALL OF THE STARS
Five Wonderful Stories of People Looking to the Heavens

Book 12: MYSTERIES OF NATURE'S LAWS
Five Striking Stories of People Investigating the Deepest Puzzles of Reality

Published by

WS Education, an imprint of
World Scientific Publishing Co. Pte. Ltd.
5 Toh Tuck Link, Singapore 596224
USA office: 27 Warren Street, Suite 401-402, Hackensack, NJ 07601
UK office: 57 Shelton Street, Covent Garden, London WC2H 9HE

National Library Board, Singapore Cataloguing in Publication Data
Name(s): Vittachi, Nury, 1958– | Cheung, Step, illustrator.
Title: The amazing quantum : five awesome stories of people who made a revolution in physics / author, Nury Vittachi ; illustrator, Step Cheung.
Other title(s): Young scientists series ; 6.
Description: Singapore : World Scientific Publishing Co Pte Ltd, 2017.
Identifier(s): OCN 969703016 | ISBN 978-981-3221-52-9 (paperback)
Subject(s): LCSH: Physicists--Juvenile literature. | Scientists--Juvenile literature. | Quantum theory--Juvenile literature. | Physics--Juvenile literature. | Science--Juvenile literature.
Classification: DDC 530.0922--dc23

British Library Cataloguing-in-Publication Data
A catalogue record for this book is available from the British Library.

All royalties received will be channelled to the National Book Development Council of Singapore (NBDCS) as a gift from the author.

First published 2017
Reprinted 2018

Printed in Singapore